# GLASS BLOWER

## MAKERS AND ARTISANS

JOSH GREGORY

Published in the United States of America by Cherry Lake Publishing Group
Ann Arbor, Michigan
www.cherrylakepublishing.com

Reading Adviser: Beth Walker Gambro, MS, Ed., Reading Consultant, Yorkville, IL
Photo Credits: © tdub_video/iStock.com, cover, 1, 5; © Benoit Daoust/Shutterstock.com, 6; © Stefan Malloch/Shutterstock.com, 8; © Yasemin Yurtman Candemir/Shutterstock.com, 9; © BalazsSebok/ Shutterstock.com, 10; © epic_images/Shutterstock.com, 11; © kaca kaca/Shutterstock.com, 13; © ramonailumuscom/iStock.com, 14; © Benoit Daoust/Shutterstock.com, 15; © Nathan Boler/ Shutterstock.com, 16; © Gabriel Pahontu/Shutterstock.com, 18; © bjones27/iStock.com, 21; © David Pineda Svenske/Shutterstock.com, 23; © WiP-Studio/Shutterstock.com, 24; © Sharon Wildie/Shutterstock.com, 27; © Raymond Well/Shutterstock.com, 28

**Cherry Lake Press** is an imprint of Cherry Lake Publishing Group.

Library of Congress Cataloging-in-Publication Data

Names: Gregory, Josh, author.
Title: Glass blower / by Josh Gregory.
Description: Ann Arbor, Michigan : Cherry Lake Publishing, [2022] | Series: Makers and artisans | Includes index. | Audience: Grades 4-6
Identifiers: LCCN 2021007801 (print) | LCCN 2021007802 (ebook) | ISBN 9781534187207 (hardcover) | ISBN 9781534188600 (paperback) | ISBN 9781534190009 (pdf) | ISBN 9781534191402 (ebook)
Subjects: LCSH: Glass blowing and working—Vocational guidance—Juvenile literature. | Blown glass— Juvenile literature.
Classification: LCC TP859 .G74 2022 (print) | LCC TP859 (ebook) | DDC 666/.122—dc23
LC record available at https://lccn.loc.gov/2021007801
LC ebook record available at https://lccn.loc.gov/2021007802

Cherry Lake Publishing Group would like to acknowledge the work of the Partnership for 21st Century Learning, a Network of Battelle for Kids. Please visit http://www.battelleforkids.org/networks/p21 for more information.

Printed in the United States of America
Corporate Graphics

## ABOUT THE AUTHOR

Josh Gregory is the author of more than 150 books for kids. He has written about everything from animals to technology to history. A graduate of the University of Missouri-Columbia, he currently lives in Chicago, Illinois.

# TABLE OF CONTENTS

# CHAPTER 1

# Blown Away

The **artisan** has a look of intense concentration as she skillfully twists and turns the long stick in her hands. At one end of the stick, a swirling, brightly colored mass slowly changes shape, almost as if by magic. It started out looking something like an egg, but it's taken on a whole new form. As the artisan pulls and pokes at her creation, it stretches like a piece of taffy. If you didn't know better, you might actually think you're watching candy being made. But you wouldn't want to eat what this artisan is making. As she continues to work, you realize she's forming a glass vase!

Glass blowers must work with their glass while it is hot.
They have a very short window of time before it cools.

Some artisans will pour molten glass into shaped molds.

People have been making glass and shaping it into all kinds of objects for a very long time. No one knows exactly when people first discovered how to create glass, but it probably happened at least 4,500 years ago. Somehow, people realized that sand melted when heated at very high temperatures. As it melts, sand turns into **molten** glass. During this phase, the glass is very hot and bloblike.

It can be formed into almost any shape. As it cools, the glass hardens into a solid object.

The earliest known glass objects were simple beads. But over time, people developed new techniques for working with glass. They use molds and forms to shape it into decorations and useful objects such as cups and bowls.

## A Long-Lasting Art Form

Glassmaking technology has advanced greatly over the centuries. Early glassmakers quickly discovered how to create new forms of glass by using different kinds of sand or by adding substances to the sand. For example, adding certain chemicals to molten glass can change the glass's color. Some varieties of sand produce glass that is perfectly clear. Others result in glass that's cloudy and hard to see through.

Modern knowledge of chemistry allows scientists and engineers to create glass with many useful properties. Today, we have everything from the heat-resistant glass used to make cookware to the extra-strong glass used to make phone screens that don't scratch easily.

Glass blowers have to be very careful. At any moment, the glass could shatter.

About 2,000 years ago, glass artisans in Syria developed a new technique. By blowing through a hollow tube inserted into a blob of molten glass, they could create a hollow pocket of air inside. It works a lot like blowing a bubble when you chew gum. By rotating the glass "bubble" and shaping it with a variety of tools, artisans created glass forms unlike anything seen before. This technique, called glass blowing, soon spread to other cultures around the world. Over time, different groups put their own spin on the process.

The longer a glass blower blows, the bigger the bubble they will create.

Murano glass figurines are world-famous. The glass blowers use 1,000-year-old techniques that started in Venice, Italy.

Artists can make beautiful glass jewelry.

Today, talented artisans continue to create amazing things using the glass blowing techniques people have used for centuries. They make beautiful and useful items such as pitchers and vases. They also use the technique to sculpt works of art. The only limits to what glass blowers can create are their imagination and skill level.

# CHAPTER 2

# Not Just Another Day at the Office

Glass blowers spend their days in a workspace filled with tools and special equipment. This space is often called a hot shop. These spaces vary from a small studio where one or two people work to a large factory where workers make drinking glasses or dishes on an assembly line. But no matter the scale of the operation, the space is sure to be hot and filled with activity.

The process of blowing glass begins by heating molten glass in a furnace that can reach temperatures well above 1,000 degrees Fahrenheit (538 degrees Celsius). The glass blower then inserts one end of a long, hollow steel pipe into the furnace and grabs a blob of molten glass. This pipe is called the blowpipe. Once enough glass is gathered on the end, the artisan transfers it to a wide,

Glory holes take a lot of energy to heat to temperature. They have special doors that help hold the heat.

flat surface made of marble or steel. This surface is called the **marver**. Using the blowpipe, the artisan gently rolls the blob of molten glass on the marver to give it a **cylindrical** shape.

By this point, the glass is already starting to cool down. As they work, glass blowers must keep the glass hot to avoid hardening. They must frequently reheat the glass in a second furnace known as a glory hole. A glory hole's working temperature is around 2,250 degrees Fahrenheit (1,232 °C).

Glass blowers have torches at their station to help sculpt
and keep the glass from cooling too fast.

The next major step is blowing a bubble into the blob of molten glass at the end of the pipe. Some blowers place one end of the pipe on a stand as they do this. Others simply hold it in their hand. They then breathe short puffs of air into the end of the pipe. As they do this, they continue to rotate the pipe. Glass blowers must keep their creation in nearly constant movement as they work. Just like keeping the glass hot, this prevents it from hardening too soon.

Glass blowers will often work in pairs.
One person will blow, while the other will shape.

Small pieces of colored glass are called frit.
They can be added to a piece to create color.

At this stage, glass blowers have several options for adding color to the glass. For example, they might roll their blob of molten glass in colored glass powder or a bowl of glass chunks. By turning the molten glass and heating it again in the glory hole, they can melt the new colors into their original pieces and swirl them around. They also can add stripes and other patterns by melting rods or other shapes of glass onto the sides of a larger piece. These rods of colored glass are called canes. The choices for adding colors and patterns to a piece of glass are nearly limitless.

Glass blowers might repeat the steps of blowing, shaping the glass on the marver, and reheating it in the glory hole several times before they get the shape right. They might continue adding more molten glass to the outside and blowing the bubble larger to increase the piece's size. Once they're satisfied, it's time to move on to the next step. The artisan, often with help from an assistant, attaches a long metal rod called a **punty** to the blown glass. The artisan then removes the blowpipe from the glass, leaving it stuck on the end of the punty.

While continuously turning the punty and occasionally reheating the glass in the glory hole, artisans use a variety of tools to add more detail to their work. They use tongs and tweezers to pinch the glass into different shapes or add texture to the surface. Flat paddles press down and flatten the glass. Artisans can get really

*Glass blowers have to be extremely careful when moving a piece, such as when transferring a piece from a blowpipe to a punty. If the piece falls or hits something, it might be ruined. The entire process may have to be started over, with hours of work wasted.*

Glass blowers use shears to help cut molten glass.

creative with this phase of the project, using any tools they find to bring their ideas to life. They also can add more pieces of molten glass to the main piece to create complex shapes. For example, they could attach another piece of glass to one side to form the handle of a pitcher. Or they could use a smaller blob of molten glass to **weld** two larger pieces of blown glass together.

Once the piece is complete, it's time to remove the punty. Then, the blower places the completed object inside an annealing oven.

This special oven starts out very hot. It's close to the temperature of the glory hole. Over a period of more than half a day, the oven very slowly cools down to room temperature. This is an important step in the process because glass can crack or break if it cools too quickly.

Finally, the artisan can put the finishing touches on the project. Sharp edges are ground and polished, and the glass is cleaned and prepared for display.

## Staying Safe

There is no way to make glass objects without using high heat and potentially dangerous tools. Broken glass is also very sharp and can easily cause cuts if not handled carefully. This means beginners must always work under the watchful eyes of a seasoned professional. Even the most experienced glass blowers often prefer to work with a partner or assistant to help avoid accidents.

Glass blowers typically wear long pants, long-sleeve shirts, and boots when they work. They might also put on heat-resistant gloves when necessary. Even though studio temperatures are very hot, this clothing helps protect against cuts, burns, and other injuries.

**Ventilation** is also an important part of glass blowing safety. Molten glass gives off gases that can be harmful to breathe.

# CHAPTER 3

# Shaping a Career

Some people work with glass as a hobby. They use it to express their creativity or fill up free time. Others are so passionate about their craft that they make it their career. Working as a full-time glass blower isn't easy. But for the right type of person, it can be very rewarding.

Like any art form, glass blowing requires a sense of creativity. If you like to experiment with shapes and colors, it could be a good fit for you. But glass blowing is more than just an art form. It also requires a great deal of physical skill. You must enjoy working with your hands if you want to make it as a glass blower. You have to be comfortable working hard, getting dirty, and practicing constantly to improve your skills.

Glass blowers may experience soreness or pain
after long days at the hot shop.

Unlike drawing, writing, making music, and many other creative activities, glass blowing can be tough for a beginner to get involved in. You can't just pick up a few supplies at the art store and start making glass at home. You need many special tools and materials, as well as a proper workplace and safety equipment. You'll also need guidance from an experienced artisan. The best way to try glass blowing is to check out classes at a local studio. Many professional glass blowers enjoy sharing their knowledge with students. Plus, teaching can provide them with extra income.

If you get serious about glass blowing, you can follow many potential paths to make it a career. Some aspiring glass blowers attend college to sharpen their skills and learn more about art.

## Use and Reuse

One of the great things about glass is that it is recyclable. All you need to do to reuse old glass is melt it down and shape it into something new. Glass blowers can always use broken glass or scrap pieces in future projects.

Glass blowers must be able to handle the heat of the hot shop.

Studying art history and getting feedback from professors or fellow artists can be a great way to grow and improve. However, college isn't a requirement to start working as a glass blower.

Many glass blowers begin their careers with an **apprenticeship**. As an apprentice, you work closely with a professional glass blower. You get to watch and learn while assisting the glass blower. Over time, you'll get to work more independently.

Artisans don't stop learning and acquiring new skills once they go pro. Instead, they strive to keep getting better and trying new things throughout their entire careers. They experiment with new

Glass blowers who manufacture goods for stores often make the same objects over and over again.

techniques and study other artists' work to get inspired. It's a life of creativity and dedication to a craft.

Of course, working as a glass blower isn't all fun and games. It's still a job, and that involves considerations beyond simply creating. Workdays can be long, and projects don't always turn out as planned. And if you work for a larger company that produces goods to be sold in stores, you might not get much chance for creativity at all. In this case, you'll have to work on more creative projects on your own time.

Many glass blowers are either self-employed or work at small, independent companies. These artisans have a little more freedom to put a personal stamp on their creations. However, they still need to consider their customers' needs and desires. Some glass blowers might sell their work at craft fairs, small shops, or online. Others might work closely with their customers to create custom pieces. These blowers need to be professional and reliable. Their work needs to be of consistent high quality.

Glass blowing isn't usually a high-paying career. Many artisans are happy to trade the chance of a high salary for the opportunity to work doing something they love. But that doesn't mean glass blowers can't make a comfortable living. Those with strong instincts for business and marketing could find a large audience for their creations. In these cases, the sky is the limit for how much a glass blower can earn. If you're thinking about a career as an artisan, it's a good idea to study the basic principles of running a business. You should also learn the ins and outs of selling things online and promoting your work on social media. These are great ways for an independent artisan to turn a passion into a thriving business.

# CHAPTER 4

# The Greats of Glass Blowing

Some glass artists have found fame and fortune. Their creations are in museums and galleries around the world, and they can even sell for millions of dollars. One of the most well-known is Dale Chihuly, whose large, colorful glass sculptures are often displayed in public places where they can be enjoyed by as many people as possible. Born in Tacoma, Washington, in 1941, Chihuly began making blown glass artwork in the 1960s. Like many glass blowers who work on large projects, he relies on a team of talented artisans to help bring his ideas to life.

In the late 1800s, Louis Comfort Tiffany became famous for his beautiful stained glass lamps, windows, and other decorative objects. He also developed a new method of coloring blown glass

Glass can become anything the artist wants.

to give it an **iridescent** appearance. Tiffany's blown glass vases and other objects remain in demand and highly valuable today.

Famous works of glass art serve as inspiration for the artisans of today and tomorrow. An artisan might start out learning to make glass objects by imitating someone else's style. But as artisans gain experience, they start to develop their own style. If you come across a work of art that really speaks to you, don't be afraid to let it influence your creations.

Dale Chihuly's blown-glass flower sculpture is
100 feet (30.5 meters) long and suspended in the air.

Whether you want to start a career as a professional glass blower or simply make things in your spare time, there's a lot to learn. Take your time, be creative, and keep trying until you get it right. But most importantly, have fun!

## Getting Inspired

You might be surprised where you find inspiration for creative projects. Glass blowers might get new ideas from looking at other artisans' creations. But they might also be inspired by simply walking around and looking at their surroundings. A unique building could give someone a new idea for the shape of a vase. Or a field of flowers could inspire a new color combination. Try carrying a notebook when you go somewhere new. That way, you can write and sketch any ideas you might have.

# Craft Activity

## Glass Blowing Up Close

It's never too early to start planning your own glass blowing projects. Form some interesting ideas and then find out if they will work in real life.

### SUPPLIES

- Colored pencils
- Paper

### STEPS

1. Use colored pencils or other art supplies to sketch out some ideas for projects. Be as detailed as you can, and don't be afraid to get wild. Think about the shapes and colors you'd like to see in real life.

2. Seek out a live demonstration by a professional glass blower. You might find these at museums, art galleries, glass workshops, or craft fairs. Bring your sketches when you go.

3. Watch the demonstration carefully and listen to what the glass blower has to say. When you get a chance, ask the glass blower if they have a moment to look at your sketches. Ask if the artisan thinks the projects would be possible to make in real life. If not, why not? If yes, how would they go about doing it?

4. Be sure to thank the glass blower for talking with you. When you get home, think about the advice you got and use it to redesign your sketches.

# Find Out More

## BOOKS

Spielman, Madison. *All About Hand-Blown Glass.* New York, NY: Time for Kids, 2004.

Spielman, Madison. *Craft It: Hand-Blown Glass.* New York, NY: Time for Kids, 2011.

## WEBSITES

**U.S. Bureau of Labor Statistics Occupational Outlook Handbook—Craft and Fine Artists**
*www.bls.gov/ooh/arts-and-design/craft-and-fine-artists.htm*
Check out official data about employment rates, average salaries, and more for professional artists.

**YouTube—Corning Museum of Glass**
*www.youtube.com/user/corningmuseumofglass/videos*
Watch dozens of videos of artisans making unique objects from glass.

# GLOSSARY

**apprenticeship** (uh-PREN-tiss-ship) an arrangement where an inexperienced worker trains with someone more experienced

**artisan** (AR-tuh-zuhn) someone who is skilled at working with their hands on a specific craft

**cylindrical** (suh-LIN-drih-kuhl) having a round, tubelike shape

**iridescent** (ear-uh-DEH-suhnt) something that appears to change color when viewed from different angles

**marver** (MAHR-vuhr) a flat surface on which hot glass is rolled, shaped, and cooled

**molten** (MOHL-tuhn) liquefied by heat

**punty** (puhn-tee) a metal rod used to work with hot glass

**ventilation** (ven-tuh-LAY-shuhn) the ability of air to flow freely within a space

**weld** (WELD) to join by heating and pressing together

# INDEX